Basildon Park

Berkshire

 **National Trust**

Decline and Resurrection

This is a story of grandeur created, dissolved and resurrected – not once, but twice.

On Friday, 13 December 1929, the Basildon Park Estate was put up for sale. The catalogue described the property enticingly as 'ripe for development'. Lot 32 offered 'An Important Speculative Lot comprising the site of Basildon House, together with its pleasure grounds'. Not for the first time, or the last, Basildon Park faced destruction.

Basildon Park was built between 1776 and 1783 for Sir FRANCIS SYKES, who had amassed a considerable fortune working for the East India Company in Bengal. Sykes had acquired the estate in 1771, in a part of Berkshire nicknamed 'the English Hindoostan' because so many of Sykes's fellow nabobs who had made money in India were settling there.

As the site is now required for other purposes, this Historical Mansion must be removed, and the owner offers for a payment of $1,000,000 to carefully take it down and re-erect it in America, in any suitable position, with certain fireplaces and banisters which have been taken away replaced by others of the same period, otherwise complete in all respects and ready for occupation as a Private Residence, or as a Museum, College Building, or Public Library.

Any patriotic American wishing to benefit his native State by presenting this imposing building is hardly likely to again meet with such an unique opportunity.

None of us like to be forgotten, and the gift of this imposing mansion would, for the expenditure of quite a moderate sum, perpetuate the name and fame of the donor for all time as a liberal and high-minded citizen of his native land.

Communications upon this matter should be addressed to the owner,

George Ferdinando, Esquire,
Basildon Park,
Berkshire,
England.

The 1929 sale brochure

Sykes commissioned John Carr of York to build a Palladian villa, with interiors in the fashionable Adam style. Carr combined a restrained use of ornament with an unerring sense of balance to create one of the most splendid Georgian houses in Berkshire.

However, soon after Basildon was built, signs of decline became evident. Some of the principal rooms were never completed, probably because Sykes was under financial pressure as he faced a clamour of corruption charges about his activities in India. Following his death in 1804, the family fortunes declined still further. The 2nd Baronet had a wayward reputation, and his son showed little interest in Basildon. The house was leased to a succession of tenants and put on the market in 1829. Sykes refused to sell for less than £100,000, and as a result failed to negotiate a deal until 1838. In the meantime, Basildon was left in the care of Sykes's steward, Mr Whitely, and his London solicitor, Mr Lake.

Basildon was eventually purchased by the Liberal MP JAMES MORRISON, who had transformed his modest haberdashery warehouse into a vast and highly successful international business, employing a philosophy of 'small profits and quick returns'. He found Basildon in a sad state. A visit by the influential garden designer John Claudius Loudon in 1834 had resulted in a less than complimentary report, whilst Alfred Morrison wrote in 1841 of the estate, 'It is in a wretched condition.'

Under Morrison's ownership, Basildon enjoyed a renaissance. He commissioned his friend the architect J. B. Papworth to complete the unfinished rooms and embellish Carr's lodges on the Oxford Road, as well as design additional new buildings for the estate. The house became a setting for Morrison's famous collection of Old Master and modern British paintings; here he welcomed friends, politicians, journalists, artists and other guests. Basildon remained in the hands of the Morrisons throughout the 19th century, but after the death of Ellen Morrison in 1910, the house was left empty except when used as an army convalescent home during the First World War. Basildon was sold in 1928, and was put back on the market for the fateful sale of 1929.

Lot 32 went to a property speculator, Mr Ferdinando, who immediately produced a brochure offering the house for demolition. In the Depression era, Ferdinando could find no takers, and the house was abandoned, having been stripped of many of its fittings such as chimneypieces, doors, doorcases and sections of plasterwork. During the Second World War the house was requisitioned, and the troops, clerks, labourers and prisoners of war billeted in and around the house caused further damage.

But the house survived, to experience its most remarkable resurrection thanks to LORD and LADY ILIFFE, who bought what was left in 1952. They restored the damaged decoration and missing fittings, and breathed new life into neglected rooms, which they furnished with appropriate Old Master pictures and historic textiles. Their achievement sent an encouraging signal to others concerned to rescue dilapidated country houses. In 1978, they generously gave the house and park, together with a fine collection of pictures and furniture and a large endowment, to the National Trust, helping to ensure that, after such a chequered past, Basildon can enjoy a brighter future.

Basildon Park from the west; by Gilbert Spencer (Back Stairs)

Saving Basildon

by Lady Iliffe, 1979

It was in 1938, the year of our marriage, that I first saw Basildon – we just drove past it, as it was empty and no sign of life inside; the park and trees looked abandoned, but I remembered how lovely it looked in the afternoon sun. Then the war engulfed us for six years, after which came the difficult post-war period, with rationing still enforced. But our mutual interest in the 18th century was by then becoming evident, and we began to think of a house in Berkshire – an old rectory for instance.

One day, in 1952, I went to look at Basildon, not thinking of it in that context, but out of sheer curiosity and interest, wondering how it had survived the war. It was just about to be de-requisitioned by the Ministry of Works. Soldiers of various nationalities and finally German prisoners of war had long since left, but there were still a few workmen billeted there. We were allowed to go inside and wander round for the first time. To say it was derelict is hardly good enough: no window was left intact, and most were repaired with cardboard or plywood; there was a large puddle on the Library floor, coming from the bedroom above, where a fire had just been stopped in time; walls were covered with signatures and graffiti from various occupants. There was one army wash-room, for six people at a time, but no other sign of modernisation. It was appallingly cold and damp. And yet, there was still an atmosphere of former elegance, and a feeling of great solidity. Carr's house was still there, damaged but basically unchanged.

Outside, thick in nettles and remnants of Nissen huts, we stumbled on old boots and pieces of sacking, thrown out of windows. We looked around in amazement, then on leaving I remember saying to a friend 'How sad, what a waste – and it could still be saved', and he said 'Why don't you?'

That is how it started. My husband agreed and we set to work. Rationing of building

Lord Iliffe, painted by Graham Sutherland in 1976

materials was still in force; permits had to be obtained; we had to keep the restoration to essential repairs, such as cutting out dry rot, and merely decorating essential rooms. It was only later that we gradually repaired the whole house. But first we had to learn more about Carr's architecture, so we made a pilgrimage to Yorkshire where most of his houses are, and looked at Harewood House, Farnley Hall, any Carr house we could find, and finally to Panton Hall in Lincolnshire, which was going to be used for storing crops, and has since then been pulled down. There we found just what we needed to repair the house, including the two marble chimneypieces now in the Dining Room and Library. The owner was delighted to do a deal, and we returned in great excitement, followed by two loaded lorries.

Carr was such a precise architect that his mahogany doors from Panton fitted exactly into the sockets of the missing Basildon ones. So we used them on the top landing, keeping the few original ones which remained at

Basildon, and were of better quality, for the reception rooms. The whole of the restoration of the centre block was over in a year and a half, with the local builder, Mr Smallbone, doing a wonderful job with his skilled craftsmen. The repairs to the two pavilions were to follow much later.

We were both determined not to overdo the restoration, and thus curtains and colour schemes had to be kept in control, so as to blend with ceilings where original colours had survived but faded. Hence the silk curtains in the Dining Room, the Octagon Room and the Hall, all date from the 18th or 19th centuries. Where new ones were unavoidable, we copied old shapes, taking them to pieces and realising how much fuller they were than modern 'drapes'. The whole household helped; the butler held the ladder while the cook and I nailed the red felt on the wall. It was fascinating and exhausting, but we were all 25 years younger!

Gradually the house filled up and we tackled the two pavilions. Thanks to modernisation of kitchen and garden implements, it was possible to keep the number of staff to the minimum, and we were lucky, on the whole, to find that they also loved the house, and did all they could for it; in fact, I do not think anybody left because it was too large or too much work.

Pictures were the main problem, and gradually we found ourselves exchanging early purchases, such as small French canvases, for larger Italian ones; they seemed to suit the house, and this explains why the Italian school of the 17th and 18th centuries dominates. It was a continuous process, and even the Mentmore sale yielded one or two items, but due to present prices we came back with coal scuttles instead of marble-topped console-tables.

After 25 very happy years in the house, my husband has handed it over to the National Trust, hoping that the Trust will protect it and its park for future generations to enjoy.

This is one of a number of original mahogany doors with their fittings to have survived Basildon's dereliction. For the top floor, the Iliffes salvaged doors from another Carr of York house, Panton Hall, which they found fitted exactly

Tour of the House

The West Front

It is not until you enter the park that you get your first sight of the long Bath stone entrance front which is among the finest late Palladian façades in England. The principal block of seven bays is dominated by a recessed Ionic portico which creates a dramatic interplay of light and shade, a favourite device of the building's architect, John Carr of York. Carr's designs for Basildon were probably inspired by Palladio's Villa Emo at Fanzolo and represent his most southerly commission.

The two flanking pavilions echo the central block in their pediments and round-headed windows. The one-storey-high walls not only link the pavilions to the main block, but also provide an ingenious screen for the four separate service courtyards that housed the domestic offices, hiding the servants from view. The north pavilion originally contained the Kitchen, Scullery and Housekeeper's Room. The south pavilion accommodated the Laundry, Wash House and Dairy. The servants slept in the rooms above. Concealed within the yards were the more unsightly domestic offices such as larders, stores for wood and coal and the privies.

The west front

The East Front

The garden front, facing the River Thames, has a much greater sense of movement than the entrance façade, thanks to the broad, bay window of the main block, which projects forward from the pavilions, another device favoured by Carr. Further contrasts are provided by the differing heights of the walls, pavilions and the central block, and the subtle breaks of plane at the corners of the pavilions. The ornament is crisply carved, and the balustrade at first-floor level ties the whole composition together.

The east front

The Loggia

Carr cleverly brought a sense of anticipation to the entrance, which was much admired. When he took his nieces to see the house in 1796, one of them recorded in her diary that the entrance was 'very singular and beautiful. You ascend into the principal storey by a double flight of steps under a beautiful Loggio of Columns.'

The central archway in the basement leads to a deeply shadowed vestibule flanked by paired Doric columns and pilasters. Ahead, the central door opened into the Lower Hall, which would have been used as the everyday family entrance, or by guests during bad weather. The principal entrance, however, is above, approached by the twin staircases on either side. A dramatic transformation takes place as one ascends into the huge, airy portico fronted by its massive Ionic columns. Inside, the Bath stone has retained its warm colour, contrasting with the weathered, silvered stone of the external façade. The portico has been described as 'a place to catch the sun', where Sir Francis Sykes may have recalled the sheltered Indian verandas of his earlier life. Carr probably designed the doors that lead into the Hall as a pair of solid panelled doors. The glazed doors were installed by Papworth in 1840.

Furnishings

Torchères decorated with bas-reliefs of classical figures. Based upon the Barberini candelabra in the Vatican Museum, which were illustrated in C. H. Tatham's *Ancient Ornamental Architecture* (1799). James Morrison probably introduced them in 1840.

Two pairs of Chinese Dogs of Fo, late 19th-century.

The west front, as engraved by George Richardson in 1797

7

The Hall

This is the first of a suite of richly decorated rooms in the centre of the house. They were used for the grand entertainments that were a regular part of country-house life in the 18th century, and their relative importance was mirrored in the quality of Carr's decoration.

However, when Lord and Lady Iliffe arrived at Basildon, they found that many of the original fittings, such as some doors and almost all the chimneypieces, were missing, and Carr's decorative schemes were in a very poor state. The first task was to dry the place out and cut out the dry rot. Only then could the interiors be repaired and coaxed back to life.

Plasterwork

The Neo-classical plasterwork ornament of the ceiling shows the influence of the Adam brothers on Carr, who had used the Rococo style in his earlier commissions. Many of the details, such as diamond-patterned bands, were taken from *The Book of Ceilings*, published in 1776 by George Richardson, who had achieved fame as Robert Adam's draughtsman. The griffins are a typical Neo-classical ornament, but may also refer to Sir Francis Sykes's Indian career, as these mythological beasts guarded all the gold of India. The work was probably carried out by William Roberts, who received regular payments, amounting to over £150, between 1777 and 1785, and who is known to have been working in the area from 1771.

The Iliffes found the ceiling more or less intact, except for a section approximately two metres square which presumably had been moved by the previous owner so that casts could be made for sale to the purchasers of other fittings that had been removed. Jackson's of London copied the plaster sphinx and replaced the missing section. The trophies of arms on the walls are a reminder that entrance halls had been used as armouries in more troubled times.

Decoration

The colouring of the ceiling, with its warm buffs, pink, lilac, green and gilded ornament, probably dates from the alterations made by

Papworth in 1840. Carr would probably have specified cooler tones.

The Iliffes had the ceiling cleaned, but not repainted, with damaged areas being recast and touched in. In order to achieve a balanced and harmonious effect, the Iliffes continued this colour scheme down the walls, which had been painted cream by the wartime occupiers. The work was supervised by their lifelong friend, the architect Winton Aldridge, and was carried out by a local firm, Smallbones of Streatley.

Doors

The doors, made from fine Spanish mahogany and attributed to Chippendale, are richly carved with a plaited pattern to the borders of the panels. They are original to the house and retain their original ormolu (gilt brass) handles and key escutcheons. They survived the wartime vandalising of the house thanks to Lord Iliffe's father who had removed seven of them to his London house at Carlton House Terrace. They were returned to Basildon in 1954.

Chimneypiece

The original white marble chimneypiece was removed in 1930 by Messrs Robersons. The Iliffes salvaged the present carved wood surround from Panton Hall in Lincolnshire, which had a very similar interior designed by Carr. Like Basildon, Panton had suffered from institutional occupation during the war. It stood empty from 1945, gradually decaying until it was demolished in 1964. The Iliffes bought two lorry loads of salvaged material from the owner, who was delighted to sell items that seemed little more than junk so that he could take his children for a holiday at the seaside.

Furniture

To find appropriate furniture for their restored house, the Iliffes frequented the many country house sales of the 1950s, acquiring fine pieces, often for modest prices.

The pair of painted side-tables with marble tops, in the style of William Kent *c.*1730, was purchased from the great sale at Ashburnham Place, Sussex, in 1953. Famous decorators of the day, such as John Fowler and Nancy Lancaster, were also at the sale, but it was the Iliffes, advised by the furniture connoisseur Francis Egerton, who recognised the potential of these two tables, which were then painted a shiny bottle green. They were restored to reveal the original surface.

The circular table with a painted top depicting putti, flowers, foliage and bacchanalian masks dates from *c.*1820.

The large painted Italian workbox with a hinged lid contains an arrangement of foliage incorporating 18th-century gilt Japanese flowers.

Ceramics

On the round table is a Wedgwood caneware (ie cane-coloured stoneware) wine-cooler, designed to hold three bottles. On the side-tables is a pair of Imari dishes celebrating the Spring Festival at Kyoto.

Textiles

The red damask curtains came from Blenheim Palace and were said to have formed part of Ince & Mayhew's scheme of decoration there in the 1760s.

Detail of William Kent-style side-tables bought in 1953

9

The Library

Carr placed the Library in the north-west corner of the house, with a door to the right (now removed) communicating directly with Sir Francis Sykes's Dressing Room, which was later described in 1828 as a 'Morning Room or adjoining study'. In the 18th century the library was regarded as a male preserve and was balanced by a corresponding suite of 'feminine' rooms, comprising Lady Sykes's bedroom and dressing rooms, in the south-west corner of the house. The apartments of the owner and his wife were separated by the main reception rooms in the centre of the house. The Iliffes continued this French-inspired arrangement: the Library formed Lord Iliffe's study; the corresponding room across the Hall was Lady Iliffe's Blue Drawing Room (now the Sutherland Room).

Ceiling

In 1946, when the house was occupied by military clerks, a fire started in the bedroom above. Scorch marks still visible on the floorboards bear witness to the collapse of the original plasterwork ceiling. All that survives is the ornament in the corners of the room. The original frieze does, however, remain decorated with pairs of griffins, a motif mirrored in the door surrounds.

Doorcases, dado and bookcases

The doorcase and the dado rail were salvaged from Panton Hall in 1952. According to Dr Gustav Waagen, who visited in the 1850s, Morrison had a particularly grand 18th-century bookcase, the front part of which consisted of 'a beautiful brown marble with shells, which is framed in black marble'. This was later sold to Mrs Ionides by Crowthers after they had stripped it from the house. After failing to find a similar replacement, Winton Aldridge designed the present bookcase using mouldings salvaged from Panton. Many of these were covered with thick accumulations of paint which all but hid the carved detail, so Smallbones rigged up a pickling plant close to the house to strip the paint off the salvaged items.

Chimneypiece

This was also salvaged from Panton, after a search had revealed parts of the missing columns buried beneath a patch of nettles in the yard. The columns are blue lapis scagliola, an imitation marble made from plaster or cement combined with colourings and stone chips. It is carefully rolled, cut and polished to replicate the veined patterns of natural marble.

Decoration

Lady Iliffe has recounted how they used the Library undecorated, with nothing but lining paper until they had decided on a suitable colour. The glowing red was achieved by painting a red on to a chrome yellow, which was then toned with a glaze made from stout. It is a particularly effective foil for the lapis blue flecked with yellow of the chimneypiece. The curtains were made by Kebles of South Audley Street, London, to a design by Winton Aldridge.

Paintings

The paintings reveal the scope and quality of the Iliffes' collection. Several are typical of the kind of Italian painting bought by 18th-century British collectors while on the Grand Tour.

Between the windows hangs the portrait of Lord Iliffe by Graham Sutherland (1903–80), which was commissioned in 1976. Lord Iliffe commented, 'My reaction when we started off was that I was a most difficult subject. My mother used to say I had no likeness.' In fact, Sutherland's sensitive treatment produced one of his most revealing portraits.

On the opposite wall hang *Rinaldo and Armida* and *The Rape of Europa* by Charles de la Fosse (1636–1716). In the first, the virgin witch Armida comes on her former enemy, the sleeping Prince Rinaldo, and falls in love with him. From Tasso's epic poem *Gerusalemme Liberata* (1580–1), which was much illustrated by artists. They were painted in the late 17th century for Ralph, Duke of Montagu by one of four French artists working on his new London home, Montagu House. They were purchased by Lord Iliffe in 1955 from Colnaghi, and accepted by HM Government in lieu of

Rinaldo and Armida; by Charles de la Fosse

The Rape of Europa; by Charles de la Fosse

Inheritance Tax and allocated to the National Trust in 1998. Between these two pictures hangs *Alexander and the Gordian Knot* by Giovanni Paolo Pannini (*c*.1692–1765/8). Alexander is told that whoever unties the cords binding the chariot will rule the world. He severs them with a single blow of his sword.

Paintings on the fireplace wall include a landscape by Jean-François Millet (1642–79) and a pair of romantic river and seascapes by Carlo Bonavia (1730–80), a pupil of Vernet. The remaining pictures include a landscape by George Lambert (1710–65) and a portrait of Lord Arran from Ashburnham Place, Sussex.

Furniture

The mahogany side-table, and the pair of carved mahogany armchairs are of the mid-18th century. The mahogany pedestal writing-desk, possibly by Chippendale, of *c*.1760 was purchased from Ditchley Park in Oxfordshire.

The gilt overmantel mirror with four caryatid figures supporting an arched top is very similar to a design for Derby House published in the Adams' *Works in Architecture* (1779). The pair of carved wooden pedestals, also in the Adam style, was purchased at the Ashburnham sale.

Clock

The Louis XV ormolu mantel clock is by Blanchin of Paris, *c*.1790.

Ceramics

On the pedestals is a pair of early 19th-century giant gourd-shaped glass bottles, later painted with amusing genre scenes and subsequently adapted as electric lamps. Other lamps are made up from 19th-century Chinese vases and a Yingqing funerary urn. The blue-and-white baluster vases are Delft, late 17th-century.

Return to the Entrance Hall and enter the Sutherland Room opposite.

The Sutherland Room

This room formed part of the suite of 'female' rooms that balance the masculine Library on the opposite side of the house. It was designed as a dressing room to serve the adjoining bedroom, and by 1840 had become a bedroom or boudoir. It was the first room occupied by the Iliffes, who moved in with only two deckchairs. It later became Lady Iliffe's sitting room. The room is now used to display some of Graham Sutherland's studies for his great tapestry, *Christ in Glory*, at Coventry Cathedral. The redecoration has been made possible by the Highfield bequest. The white marble chimneypiece is one of the two original ones which remained.

Graham Sutherland's Tapestry for Coventry Cathedral

by Lord Iliffe, 1989

On the night of 14 November 1940, the centre of Coventry was bombed and burned all night. The next morning, the 14th-century cathedral was a charred ruin; so, incidentally, was our family newspaper. The Provost picked up two fallen beams and had them fixed in the form of a cross to an improvised altar and there held his service in the open air, the roof having collapsed, saying: 'Coventry will live again'.

Coventry did live; the cathedral was rebuilt – and so was the newspaper. It was decided not to restore the 14th-century structure but to leave it as a ruin and to build a modern cathedral by its side, employing the best of modern artists. Sir Basil Spence was chosen as architect. Graham Sutherland was asked to design a tapestry, to be hung in the chancel, behind the altar. It was to be 78 feet high by 39 feet wide, the largest in the world. Because of its size, and the artist's wish that it should be woven in one piece, it was eventually decided to employ the firm of Pinton et Felletin in France. There it was worked on a vast horizontal frame, twelve weavers sitting side by side. To survey the finished work, Sutherland had to climb up a ladder and look down at it. It took almost three years to complete, but in May 1962 it was ready for the consecration and now hangs in all its splendour in the new cathedral.

The studies in the Sunderland Room are some of those done by Graham Sutherland while he was working out his final design; they were never intended for a bedroom, of course, but they are of such quality that they would go anywhere and we put them here because of security and because the light can be controlled. They are extremely fragile and being watercolours, they would fade if exposed to strong light; also here, their impact is not diminished by other paintings and objects.

How they came to be at Basildon is a long story and I can only give the outline of it in a limited space. Sutherland gave the studies (the word he told me he preferred) to his wife Kathleen, and they looked for a buyer, possibly from the Midlands, who might like to acquire them and keep them together as a whole. I became that person and was able to present them, *in toto*, to the Herbert Art Gallery in my native city of Coventry. A friend had alerted me that they were on offer in a London gallery – I was there next morning and found 165 studies of differing sizes. One could not help being impressed by their strength and vitality. I then went to see Lord Clark, a well-known connoisseur, to hear his assessment. I told him of my thought for Coventry and he said, 'Yes, they are very important, they should be kept together and a nucleus should always be on display, showing how the design evolved'.

That nucleus is on permanent display in the Herbert Art Gallery in Coventry and, with the exception of a small loan to the cathedral, the rest of the collection is now lent to the National Trust at Basildon, where it gives me great pleasure to see them.

It was inevitable that Sutherland and I should meet, with so many interests in common; but it was in the South of France that our friendship flourished. He and Kathleen lived part of the year above Menton, where he had his studio. My wife and I spent many holidays nearby – we often met and it was here that he painted the portrait which now hangs in the Library.

(Right) Graham Sutherland's study for the face of Christ in his Christ in Glory *tapestry in Coventry Cathedral*

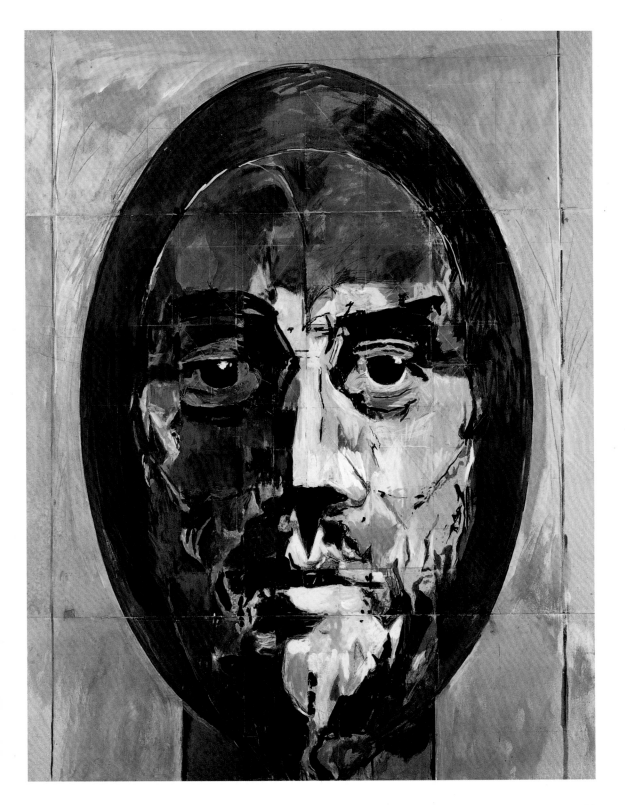

The Great Staircase

This is one of Carr's most monumental interiors, providing a formal link between the Hall and the Dining Room and Octagon Room. Carr used a similar form of top-lit staircase at Tabley House in Cheshire and Constable Burton Hall in Yorkshire, but neither matches his skilful handling of architecture, space and light at Basildon.

Staircase

The staircase is cantilevered from the wall, rising to the galleried landing above. When looking from below, you get glimpses through the archways into the vaulted bedroom corridor. The wrought-iron balustrade is decorated with medallions of putti and classical figures in moulded lead. The pattern is exactly the same as James Wyatt's staircase at Heveningham Hall, Suffolk, built in 1780–4, perhaps because Carr employed the same smith. During the restoration of 1952–4, missing and damaged sections were replaced, ingeniously using aluminium for the casts of the new medallions.

Ceiling

In the late 1940s, the Ministry of Works caretaker stole the lead from the staircase roof, causing the timbers to rot and the roof to collapse. The Ministry repaired the damage, but installed a new flat ceiling rather than Carr's original vault.

Plasterwork

The Neo-classical themes established in the Hall are continued in the delicate plasterwork on the walls of the Staircase Hall and under the two galleries, which are supported by scrolling brackets. Some of the medallions were removed by Mr Ferdinando and replaced, although most of the decoration survived the military occupation of the building as the room was boarded up. The brackets supporting the galleries were strengthened in 1978, and were recast from the originals.

Picture

The portrait of Lady Iliffe is by Frank O. Salisbury c.1942.

Furniture

The lantern hanging in the centre of the room is from Overton Park in Clwyd, for which it was supplied in October 1830. It is supported by a chain on a winding mechanism that allows it to be lowered for cleaning.

The pair of painted urns on pedestals is from Fawley Court in Buckinghamshire, only a few miles away down the River Thames. They may have been designed by James Wyatt, who remodelled the interior of that house in 1771. *The jardinière and stand* on the Adam-style gilt table, as well as the Adam-style painted pedestals on the staircase, are from Brockenhurst Park in Hampshire. *The painted planters* on the staircase are from Ashburnham Place.

(Left) Carr's Neo-classical plasterwork decorates the walls of the Great Staircase

(Right) The Great Staircase

The Dining Room

'A subdued tint pervaded every part of the chamber:
the ceiling was painted in grey tinted frescoes of a
classical and festive character, and the side table,
which stood in a recess supported by four columns,
was adorned with choice Etruscan vases.'

The Dining Room, as described in Disraeli's novel
Henrietta Temple (1837)

This was designed as the Dining Room, despite
being placed so far from the kitchen in the
North Pavilion. There would have been much
to-ing and fro-ing by footmen as they ferried
food on its circuitous route across the foot of
the Great Staircase to the back stairs and the
Dining Room, where it would have been
placed on the sideboard behind the screen
before being served. But Sir Francis Sykes
would have used the Dining Room only rarely,
for great occasions and entertainments. Family
meals would have been taken in the smaller
room (now the Green Drawing Room) at the
head of the side stairs.

The room has since seen many changes.
In 1845 James Morrison commissioned David
Brandon to make radical alterations. These were
dismantled and sold before the Iliffes commissioned John Fowler to repaint the room as a
drawing room in 1952–4. They later returned to
using it as a dining room.

The screen of columns is made of painted
plaster on a wooden frame. Since 1952, the
deteriorating scagliola columns imitating dark
red porphyry were overlayed with marble effect.

Ceiling

The complex geometrical pattern of Carr's
gently coved ceiling was again indebted to the
work of the Adam brothers and George
Richardson. In particular, the central wreath
adorned with putti emerging from acanthus
fronds is a design that can be found in
Richardson's *Book of Ceilings*.

The ceiling lunettes and medallions were
originally fitted with elegant classical allegories
painted in grisaille (ie shades of grey) by
Theodore de Bruyn (1730–1804), who was paid
£115 in 1783–4. In 1845 Morrison replaced
them with darker polychrome panels depicting

The Dining Room

The Dining Room chimneypiece is decorated with panels of superb scagliola inlay featuring a bouquet of roses (opposite) and Italian fantasy landscapes (above)

scenes from Dante's *Divine Comedy* encircled by explanatory inscriptions.

Between the two world wars, Mr Ferdinando removed the painted panels, along with the chimneypiece, doors, doorcases and mirrors. They were sold to the Waldorf Astoria Hotel in New York where they were used in a much-altered form to create the so-called 'Basildon Room'. By the 1950s, nearly every run of moulding and cornice in the Dining Room had a foot or so missing.

The present ceiling and the wall-medallions were painted in 1991–2 by Alec Cobbe in the spirit of de Bruyn's originals. By kind permission of Lord Harewood, the central roundels were based on those at Harewood House in Yorkshire, another house by Carr. The depic-

tion of three of the nine Muses – from the window end, Erato (poetry), Melpomene (tragedy) and Thalia (comedy) – recalls Lord Iliffe's literary interests and his lifelong connection with Stratford-upon-Avon.

Walls

Much of Carr's plasterwork survives, with its characteristic patterns of loops and bows along the top of each wall panel.

Chimneypiece

The chimneypiece was salvaged from Panton Hall. The extremely fine scagliola inlay, with its bouquet of pink and white roses in the central tablet and the enchanting landscapes in the friezes above each column, is probably the work of Domenico Bartoli.

Doors and doorcases

Much of the joinery apart from the original doors, was also salvaged from Panton Hall.

Textiles

The early 19th-century silk damask curtains were purchased at the Ashburnham Place sale. Reusing old curtains in this manner was then a fairly new idea. John Cornforth commented in *Country Life* that it 'is so unusual that it deserves stressing because it adds a great deal to the success of the house through giving it a settled look that could not have been achieved with new ones'.

Furniture

The pair of mahogany urns on pedestals either side of the chimneypiece came originally from Ham House near Richmond and were probably made for the 5th Earl of Dysart in 1775. They retain their original brass taps and linings and unusual ormolu handles in the shape of satyrs' masks.

The modern dining-table is surrounded by a set of chairs in the style of Chippendale, produced c.1900. *The pair of early 18th-century mahogany side-tables* with marble tops on either side of the single window is in the style of William Kent.

The steel and brass grate and fender are in perfect harmony with the rest of the room's

Neo-classical character and were purchased in 1956 at the sale of Brockenhurst Park.

Ceramics and glass

The Chinese Export armorial porcelain dates from 1765–70 and bears the arms of Francis Sykes before he was created a baronet in 1781 and was probably ordered before he left India. The porcelain is of two slightly differing shapes, suggesting that it was ordered in two lots. The crest bears a lady of Bengal holding a rose, above an oval armorial. The motto is 'SAPIENS QUI ASSIDUUS' ('He is wise who is industrious'). It was acquired by the National Trust in 1987 thanks to generous donations from Lord Iliffe, the National Art Collections Fund and National Trust Associations. Further pieces were acquired in 1999.

The glassware includes the green rummers (large short-stemmed drinking glasses) of c.1825, Irish wine glasses of c.1795, the English port glasses of c.1790, George IV water glasses, a pair of 19th-century Waterford bonbon dishes and a pair of late Regency ship's decanters.

The Octagon Drawing Room

The Octagon Drawing Room

'Ferdinand thought that he had never in his life entered so brilliant a chamber. The lofty walls were covered with an Indian paper of vivid fancy, and adorned with several pictures which his practised eye assured him were of great merit. The room, without being inconveniently crowded, was amply stored with furniture, every article of which bespoke a refined and luxurious taste: easy chairs of all descriptions, most involving couches, cabinets of choice inlay, and grotesque tables covered with articles of vertu; all those charming infinite nothings, which a person of taste might some time back have easily collected during a long residence on the continent.

A large lamp of Dresden china was suspended from the painted and gilded ceiling.'

Disraeli on the Octagon Drawing Room in the 1830s; from his novel, *Henrietta Temple*

'What a casket to enclose pictorial gems!' James Morrison's enthusiastic first reaction to Basildon encouraged him to turn this into a Picture Room, where he could hang the best Old Master paintings from his collection. (Carr had never finished decorating the room for Sir Francis Sykes.) By 1850, it had become a gallery of British art. When Dr Waagen visited in 1857, he noted that the room was 'decorated with a series of pictures by the most distinguished modern English painters', including works by Turner, Constable, Hogarth and

Richard Wilson. The Iliffes followed Morrison's example and used this room to hang some of the finest paintings from their own collection.

Ceiling

The ornate frieze and heavy ceiling, with its recessed panels painted in polychrome on parchment, are in the Italian 16th-century style. They were designed by Papworth in 1840 and preserve their original plasterwork and gilding.

Walls

In Morrison's time, the walls were covered with purple velvet, whilst early 20th-century photographs show thick bands of gilt papier-mâché ornament in the angles of the rooms. In 1954 the Iliffes, faced with bare walls, decided to line them with red felt, a colour particularly popular in the 18th century as a background for paintings. Lady Iliffe has described how she and the cook put up the red felt themselves.

Paintings

The series of paintings representing God the Father and Saints Peter, Paul, Matthew, John

St Matthew; by Pompeo Batoni

the Evangelist, Thomas, Andrew and James the Less were painted by Pompeo Batoni (1708–87). They were acquired by Lord Iliffe and, as with much of his collection, they reflect a post-war revival of interest in later Italian subject paintings. In the 18th century, Batoni was most popular among British Grand Tour visitors to Rome as a portraitist, but he also established a leading reputation for his historical and religious canvasses painted in the grand manner.

This series, originally comprising twelve pictures, was commissioned by Conte Cesare Merenda, who built up a collection of 30 paintings by Batoni which was displayed in his new gallery in the Palazzo Merenda at Forlì. The paintings were a relatively unusual commission for a secular setting, and were painted between 1740 and 1743. They remained in the Merenda collection until after the Second World War.

The other pictures in the room are by Giovanni Battista Pittoni (1687–1767) and depict *Cleopatra and the Pearl*, *The Death of Lucretia* and *Venus giving alms to Aeneas*.

St Paul; by Pompeo Batoni

Furniture

The monumental pair of Neo-classical gilt pier-tables and mirrors of the 1780s may not have been designed *en suite*, but remained together at Brockenhurst Park until they were sold off separately in 1956. Lord and Lady Iliffe subsequently acquired both pieces independently, reuniting them again in their present position.

The tables have spectacular marquetry tops, supported by female figures based on those on the Erechtheum on the Acropolis at Athens. The width of the mirrors suggests that they were meant to hang either side of a fireplace, rather than between windows, as was usual. The winged griffins and the ram's heads in the cresting echo furniture from the music room at Brockenhurst, and the ewers with dolphin handles are derived from the Theatre of Marcellus in Rome, a source used by the architect and designer William Chambers.

The pair of bronze and ormolu candelabra on the tables is said to have come from the Austrian Imperial collection and is probably the work of the greatest Parisian maker of the Empire period, Pierre-Philippe Thomire (1751–1843).

The set of eight mahogany armchairs in the Gothic style was designed by William Porden for Eaton Hall in Cheshire in about 1810.

The pair of tripod candlestands is carved with ram's masks and close in style to designs by Robert Adam. *The large Regency chandelier* is suspended from the central rosette designed by Papworth.

The 19th-century Erard grand piano was made for Mrs Dering of Baddesley Clinton in Warwickshire (also National Trust), and was

purchased at the sale of the contents in 1940 for £10. It then cost £15 to restore it.

Textiles

The pair of large pelmet boards with large scrolling brackets was bought from Ashburnham and probably dates from the 1820s. Lady Iliffe skilfully united them with earlier silk damask curtains with elaborate silk fringes, supplied by Ince & Mayhew in 1773 for the Grand Cabinet at Blenheim.

The octagonal carpet is hand-tufted in the Savonnerie style.

The marquetry tops of the pier-tables are supported by female figures inspired by the Erechtheum on the Acropolis at Athens

A Neo-classical pier-glass and table in the Octagon Drawing Room

The Green Drawing Room

The Sykeses, the Morrisons and the Iliffes all used this as a breakfast room. It is very much on the family side of the house, originally with no direct access to the adjoining Octagon Drawing Room, which was a part of the more formal and public 'circuit' rooms to the north.

Ceiling

Carr's ceiling is very close to Plate IV in Richardson's *Book of Ceilings*. Particularly close are the rectangular bands of ornament at each end, with the heads of Roman emperors depicted in profile. The painted colour scheme is a rare example of surviving 18th-century paintwork. The picking-out in pink and green without gilding is very similar to the colour schemes indicated in the few contemporary hand-tinted copies of Richardson's work.

Walls

The damask on the walls recently came from a set of Edwardian curtains once at Englefield House in Berkshire.

Chimneypiece

The white marble chimneypiece is original to the house. It may be by the sculptor Richard Westmacott the Elder, to whom Sir Francis Sykes made payments in 1782–3.

Paintings

The landscape paintings grouped here reflect Lord Iliffe's fondness for Italianate themes, and echo the view across the park and the Thames valley which can be seen from the windows.

On the left, as one enters the room, are two arcadian landscapes by Jan van Bloemen, known as Orizzonte (1662–1749). The landscape on the other window wall is by the Dutch artist Frederick de Moucheron (1638–86). The very large painting of *Rebecca at the Well* is by Sebastiano Galeotti (1676–1746). The patriarch Abraham's servant Eliezer, in his search for a suitable wife for his master, comes across Rebecca drawing water at the well.

Furniture

Below the Orizzonte landscapes are *two parquetry commodes* with mid-18th-century marble tops which are probably Neapolitan. The third commode, also of continental origin, has two inlaid panels of *vernis Martin* (a form of japanning on wood), depicting cupids at play.

The settee in the centre of the room, with two armchairs *en suite*, are in the Louis XVI style and came from Lord Ellesmere's collection at Bridgewater House in London. *The long settee* against the wall is English, but in the French taste, and is similar to pieces made by Thomas Chippendale for Windsor Castle.

The two pole-screens frame tapestry panels of birds which were probably made at the Fulham Manufactory in the 1750s. They are similar to a set of three made by Chippendale for Dumfries House in Argyllshire in 1759. The three carved and gilt pelmet boards are of a similar date.

Return to the Staircase Hall and climb the stairs to the second floor. Walk along the landing past the top of the side stairs.

The Crimson Bedroom

The Crimson Bedroom is one of the range of bedrooms and dressing rooms on the south side of the house, which were used by the family and were served by the side stairs. Those to the north were a series of guest apartments approached by the Great Staircase which were known as the 'Regent's side' – a reference to a visit made by the Prince Regent in 1813 in the time of the third Sir Francis Sykes.

Many of the rooms on this floor retain their original cornices, although the doors, doorcases and fire-surrounds were missing when the Iliffes took on Basildon. Replacements came from Panton, and such was Carr's precision that they fitted perfectly. According to Aldridge, 'they fitted like a glove', and the builders 'didn't even have to redrill the screw holes'. There is no trace of the 'Indian' wallpaper mentioned in the 1829 sale catalogue, which Sir Francis Sykes would have obtained through his position in the East India Company. (Confusingly, this wallpaper would actually have been Chinese.) The current Coles wallpaper was put up in the 1950s.

Furniture

The room is now named after the state bed, with its original crimson damask hangings, window curtains and accompanying suite of furniture, which were purchased by the Iliffes at the Ashburnham sale. One of the best surviving examples of William IV-style upholstery, the bed probably dates from 1829, when extensive alterations were made to Ashburnham Place by Lewis Vulliamy. Although no documentary evidence survives, the high quality of the swags, rosettes and fringes suggest they were made by a prominent London craftsman such as George Morant, who was appointed upholsterer to William IV in 1830. The fine sheets came from Lady Wolverton's sale.

The rug was handmade by Lady Iliffe. The design incorporates flowers and shrubs from the garden at Basildon, as well as Lady Iliffe's initials and the date.

Ceramics

Porcelain includes 18th-century Chinese bowls and saucers, and inkstand and tray, possibly by Coalport in a Sèvres style *c.*1870, and a Copeland Spode washstand.

The Crimson Bedroom

The Bamboo Bedroom

The original frieze by Carr survives, and the carved wooden chimneypiece, doors and door-cases were brought from Panton Hall.

Furniture

The early 19th-century bed, with its tester and end posts carved and painted to resemble bamboo, came from Stoneleigh Abbey, Warwickshire. A disastrous fire there, and subsequent flooding caused by the heat melting the lead water pipes, meant that many items were sold off to pay for repairs. The bed-hangings were damaged, and replaced by Lady Iliffe, although the fringe was rescued, washed and put back.

The pair of Chinese figures are 19th-century medicine dolls, used by patients to indicate their symptoms to their doctor.

Pictures

The oriental theme is continued in the aquatints either side of the overmantel glass, which are from Thomas and William Daniell's *Oriental Scenery*. The Daniells made an immense set of views of Indian monuments, which were published between 1795 and 1808. One of these scenes inspired the wallpaper recently used to decorate the Breakfast Room.

(Above) This 19th-century Chinese doll was used by patients to indicate their symptoms. It has been converted into a lamp

(Left) One of Thomas and William Daniell's aquatints of the monuments of India

(Right) The Shell Room

The Dressing Room

Set back behind the columns of Carr's loggia, this is the best place from which to view the finely carved Roman Ionic capitals, which were probably based on engravings by Piranesi. The frieze and the small cast-iron fire grate are original.

The Regency lit bateau (boat-shaped bed) is draped with muslin hangings in an Anglo-Indian style copied from contemporary paintings and drawings. The small 'empire' seat was donated to a wartime sale to raise funds for the Red Cross and St John's fund by Lord Anglesey, and purchased for Lady Iliffe by her father-in-law.

The framed piece of white satin embroidered with sprays of wild flowers and ribbons, *c.*1725–50, has been kindly lent by Mr and Mrs M. C. Parkinson.

The Shell Room

But when thy fond description tells
The beauties of this grott divine;
What miracles are wrought by shells,
Where nicest taste and fancy join …

To Lady Fane, on her Grotto at Basildon
Mr Graves, 1746

These lines celebrate the shell grotto created by the widow of Sir Henry Fane at the dower house on the Basildon estate, where she moved after the sale of the main house to Sir Francis Sykes in 1771. Decorating rooms with shells was a popular lady's amusement in the late 18th century. The Basildon grotto attracted many visitors in its day, but was said to have been 'disowned by an improved and purer taste' by the 1790s.

The present decoration was made in an 18th-century spirit by Gordon Davies in 1978. It was designed to provide a backdrop for the large collection of land and sea shells, many of considerable rarity, that was amassed by Lord Iliffe's mother, Charlotte, whose portrait also hangs in the room. In 1945 Lady Iliffe bought the important collection of the Rev. E. G. Alderson, which forms the core of the present display.

Set back behind the Loggia in the centre of the west front, this room, may originally have been used as an upstairs sitting room.

Lady Iliffe's Bedroom

This is the only bedroom to have a bed alcove and was obviously intended as the principal bedroom on the guest side of the house. When Lady Iliffe first moved to Basildon, it was impossible to enter the room because of fire damage to the floor and the Library ceiling below.

Furniture

This includes a Chippendale-style mahogany break-front bookcase, and a modern shell mirror made by Mr Davies as a present for Lady Iliffe.

Ceramics

Porcelain converted into lamps includes a Chinese Kangxi blue-and-white baluster vase, a pair of Staffordshire groups. Other pieces include the Derby plates, dish and stand painted with botanical specimens, *c.*1780, a pair of Staffordshire candlesticks, and a pair of classical-form vases decorated with scenes from the story of Paul and Virginie (a popular 19th-century French romantic novel set in Mauritius) and a mid-19th-century Minton wash-stand set.

Walk through the vaulted corridor, which has plaster-work typical of Carr's work. Through the open arches, you can look down on the Great Staircase.

The Green Chintz Room

Paintings

The portraits in this room belong to Viscount
Dillon and are lent to the National Trust at
Basildon by agreement with the trustees of the
Dillon Trust.

Furniture

The Green Chintz Room was named after the
hangings on the domed bed (a type known as a
lit à la Polonaise), which was purchased from
Ditchley Park, Oxfordshire. It was made in the
1790s for the 12th Viscount Dillon. The gold-
painted framework is original, although the
hangings were replaced in about 1930, when
Mr and Mrs Ronald Tree commissioned the
Parisian upholsterers Boudin to make new
glazed and painted chintz hangings for the bed
and matching window curtains. The curtains
incorporate the remains of the older fabric and
represent a fine example of a skill that was
becoming increasingly rare in the 20th century.

Ceramics

Pieces include a 19th-century Chinese
Dog of Fo, a late 19th-century Minton
wash-stand set, a Belleek shell-pattern
tea service and a pair of blue Paris pot-
pourri vases, *c.*1840.

*Walk along the landing and down the side
staircase to the Lower Hall.*

The Side Staircase

This was for use by the family rather
than servants, who would have taken the
tiny spiral staircase nearby. Very little of
either Carr's or Papworth's decoration
remains in this area. The highly decorative glazed lantern incorporating
garlands and rams' heads could not be
saved because of dry rot damage.

Detail of the L'Hindoustan *panoramic
wallpaper in the Garden Room, designed by
Pierre Mongin in 1807*

The Lower Hall

The Lower Hall was the everyday family
entrance to the house. The frieze and ceiling
panels, bordered with platted patterns, are
typical Carr features. However, his original
columns were removed, presumably for sale,
in the 1930s and replaced with the present
Corinthian columns and pilasters, which are
made from composition.

An arch on the central axis of the house leads
to an inner vestibule with rounded walls and a
pair of niches at the far end. On the walls are
shown views of other houses by Carr of York,
including Panton Hall, which provided so many
doorcases, doors and chimneypieces for
Basildon. On the opposite wall are some of the
other houses built by 'nabobs' of the East India
Company on their return to England.

The two white marble pedestals on either
side of the arch to the vestibule are part of the
chimneypiece carved by W. G. Nicholl for the
Octagon Drawing Room about 1840 during the
Papworth renovation.

The Angkor Wat mural in the Servants' Hall was painted by Michael Dillon in 1999

The Garden Room

This octagonal room, with an inner circle of columns in the centre of the east front, was designed by Carr as a summer breakfast room, with doors leading straight out on to the garden. Samuel Wyatt adopted a very similar arrangement at Doddington in Cheshire. By 1829 it had become a billiard room, which it seems to have remained throughout the 19th century. As with the Lower Hall, the original Doric columns were removed by Mr Ferdinando and replaced with the present Ionic columns. However, Carr's Doric frieze remains above.

The panoramic wallpaper was made by the French firm of Zuber, which since 1797 has been hand-printing decorative wallpapers at its factory in Rixheim in Alsace, using the original wooden blocks. The design, called 'L'Hindoustan' was created for the firm in 1807 by the painter Pierre Mongin, who had never been to India, but instead based his design on the Indian views of Thomas and William Daniell. He redrew their designs, using parkland of a decidedly European character as a background for the more exotic flora, fauna and costume of India. The printing process involved the use of up to 1,265 wood blocks and 85 colours. Two complete sets of the panoramic view were used to decorate the room.

The Servants' Hall

The room leading from the north-west corner of the Lower Hall which now forms part of the tea-room was originally the Servants' Hall.

Michael Dillon, Lady Iliffe's nephew, decorated it in 1999. The exotic eastern scenes, a reminder of Sir Francis Sykes's career in the East India Company, are inspired by the temple of Angkor Wat, which Lord and Lady Iliffe visited during a journey round the world.

The Garden and Park

When the Iliffes moved to Basildon, the garden and park were in as derelict a state as the house. The previous 30 years had been unkind. The sale catalogue of 1929 described woodland well stocked with mature beech, ash and oak trees, and kitchen gardens equipped with heated houses devoted to growing tomatoes, cucumbers, carnations, vines, peaches and ferns. When the purchaser, Mr Ferdinando, was unable to sell his speculative acquisition, he retained a skeleton garden staff. His son remembers the 'wonderful gardens' and the orchids, peaches and other abundant fruit and vegetables that were produced.

Wartime requisition sealed the fate of the garden, which fell into dereliction as tank drivers trained for battle in the park and prisoners of war were held in nissen huts. The Iliffes faced swathes of dense grass, nettles, ivy and bramble, which threatened to breach the very walls of the house. Everything was over-grown: the balustrade on the terrace was damaged; mature trees were lost and self-seeded weeds and scrub encroached upon the pot-holed drive. The park and its woodland were churned and rutted with tank tracks, and littered with fallen, rotting timber, Nissen huts, rolls of barbed wire and oil drums.

The Iliffes immediately set about repairing the landscape. Between 1952 and 1955, the areas around the house were cleared. Lawns were re-seeded and new borders were planted. In 1964 the courtyards were paved with bricks rescued from the derelict glasshouses in the kitchen gardens, and in 1967 the pleasure grounds were cleared and replanted to restore the few surviving remains of the original shrubbery.

Tour of the Garden

The Pleasure Grounds

When Sir Francis Sykes built Basildon, the park came right up to the east side of the house in the natural style popularised by 'Capability' Brown. To the north of the house, on ground sloping down to the main drive, a 'beautiful Lawn and Flower Garden' were concealed by trees. A description published in 1801 noted that 'The grounds are disposed with much taste' and that 'the gardens are well furnished with aromatic shrubs …'. The sale catalogue of 1829 described a garden 'most tastefully disposed with beds of the choicest Plants &c., and the walks shaded with highly ornamental Trees and Shrubberies'. Just as he chose a fairly conventional style for his house, Sykes probably accepted contemporary wisdom concerning the planting of his pleasure

The park from the air

grounds, incorporating a shrubbery planted with a variety of trees, shrubs and flowers arranged in irregular clumps in order to provide a diversity of foliage. Borders would have been planted up to a standard formula, which recommended that the tallest plants should be in the centre, surrounded by a gradual fall in height to the smallest plants at the edge.

For Morrison, J. B. Papworth enlarged and possibly replanted the pleasure grounds. Morrison also added a rose garden with a thatched 'umbrello', or shaded seat, in the centre. In 1993–4, the National Trust reinstated the gravel paths that intersected this area, and reintroduced the umbrello.

The Parterre

In the early 19th century, Regency landscape designers advocated the integration of gardens with the house itself, suggesting, for example, that windows and doors should open directly on to the lawns. Morrison laid out a parterre on the east front with a balustraded terrace walk at the far end. This also acted as a ha-ha. After Morrison quarrelled with Papworth in 1843, he consulted William Nesfield, and for advice on planting, Edward Kemp, who had worked with Joseph Paxton. The terrace and balustrade were probably designed by David Brandon.

The pair of carved stone dogs on the north side of the parterre (which is now lawn) is based on the famous marble Antique statue known as the 'Dog of Alcibiades' (now in the British Museum). Alcibiades (c.450–404 BC) was a vain and uncompromising general and politician who became the talk of Athens when he cut the tail off his uncommonly large and beautiful dog. He did this, he claimed, to give Athenians something to talk about other than himself. Modelled on a Molossian, an ancestor of the modern mastiff, the marble statue is thought to have been a Roman copy of a Greek bronze original; it was frequently copied in stone in the 18th and 19th centuries. Morrison bought this pair in Italy in 1845–6, on the advice of the sculptor Giuseppe Leonardi.

The pair of stone dogs on the parterre was inspired by the 'Dog of Alcibiades', one of the most famous sculptures of classical antiquity (now in the British Museum)

Apart from the two statues of Greek goddesses, the other garden ornaments, including the set of four late 18th-century urns carved with festoons of drapery and satyrs' masks, were bought at the Ashburnham Place sale by the Iliffes. With the advice of Lanning Roper, they also laid out the small formal garden in front of the south pavilion with beds of old-fashioned roses edged with lavender, and with a giant Coade stone vase in the centre.

The Early Park

The first visual record of the park is a map of 1762 by John Rocque, which indicates a manor house surrounded by a small formal garden enclosed within a deer-park, which largely defined the boundary of the subsequent park. The park as we see it today, especially the boundary planting, reflects the work of Sir Francis Sykes. It is contemporary with the present house, and although little documentary evidence has survived, its structure can still be discerned.

Basildon lies on the right bank of the Thames. When Joseph Farington made this aquatint in 1793, the surrounding parkland was laid out informally in the style of 'Capability' Brown

The Park in the 18th Century

In 1778 Sir Francis Sykes paid £52 10s to 'Capability' Brown, whose account book for that year describes 'Journeys and plans for kitchen garden, etc'. There is little other evidence to confirm Brown's involvement in the park. However, later accounts and maps certainly indicate the existence of a landscape laid out according to Brownian principles, which may have been the work of his many imitators. William Angus, in his *Seats of the Nobility* (1799), describes a landscape in which 'the park abounds with deer, which gives an enlivening beauty to the surrounding landscape. The whole of the grounds are laid out with great judgement, and have many local advantages, which are pleasingly adapted to the elegance of the Mansion.'

Nineteenth-century maps indicate thickened perimeter plantings with undulating edges; carefully created and placed clumps of trees scattered through open parkland to give vistas from the house; and a principal drive hidden within a plantation to shield the visitor's view of the mansion until the whole façade could be seen. The manor house was demolished and replaced with an enclosure for Carr's stables, and walled gardens and orchards were established.

Many of the trees planted by Sykes survive today, particularly in the clumps of limes, beeches and chestnuts, along with a number of venerable cedars. The National Trust has restored the park and plantations to reflect this design by replanting clumps and belts, and clearing areas of commercial timber to reopen the vistas.

The Park in the 19th Century

The park was in a neglected state when James Morrison purchased Basildon. He employed Papworth to work not only on the mansion, but also on the wider landscape. In 1842, Papworth was advising Morrison, that although the house required a grand setting, it should not sit isolated in an expanse of lawn, but should blend with the surrounding landscape and plantations through the use of shrubberies.

Papworth admired the existing landscape and did very little to alter its structure: 'My object is to increase what it has there already – extending the Grass – without too much effecting the appearance of the Hanging wood, & to leave clumps & good trees – singly or otherwise, as park furniture & embellishment.' He advocated preserving clumps of oak and elm, oak and hollies and as many thorns as possible, warning that 'it is better to cut down too little than too much at once'.

Papworth added some tree clumps to the south of the stables and offered considerable advice on the planting of trees suitable for the park. These included oaks, elms and Spanish chestnuts, with firs or larches to be 'mixed as nurses' and cut down when the other trees became more beautiful. He proposed opening up vistas of the distant landscape, as well as creating views of the house from the park.

Papworth planted evergreens and forest trees to screen the eastern boundary of the park from the Great Western Railway, the construction of which caused Morrison much aggravation. The pleasure grounds were also extended to meet the new line of the main drive from the Oxford lodges, which was designed to rise gently up the hill and offer a glimpse of the house over the newly dressed brow of the slope.

Papworth built new lodges and cottages, and designed the railway bridge with them in mind. He carefully explained how the Pangbourne Cottage should sit not only in the direct line of view through the railway bridge arch, but also to be 'very picturesque and attractive to the Railroad passengers'.

The Oxford Lodges

Papworth's last major job for Morrison was in 1842, when he embellished Carr's small octagonal lodges and gates that flank the main drive on the Reading to Oxford road. Originally, these were almost identical to those Carr had designed for Denton Park in Yorkshire. The change in the colour of the stone above their round-headed windows indicates their original height, which Papworth increased by a third. He also added rectangular panels carved with garlands and lion masks just below the parapet, turning the lodges into miniature versions of the Tower of the Winds in Athens, one of the most frequently copied classical buildings. Papworth also heightened the gate-piers and designed elaborate ornaments of cast stone: huge baskets of fruit crowned with pineapples and each held aloft by four putti. The design was based upon lead ornaments made by Van Nost for the Flower Pot Gate at Hampton Court in 1700.

The Stables

Carr's stables stood immediately in front of the mansion on the site of the old manor house. Morrison had them demolished, probably because they blocked views from the loggia on the west front of the house. The site of the new stables was near to the kitchen garden, hidden from the house in a dip to the north of the main drive.

Morrison turned to Papworth for his new stables, but disagreement over their design was symptomatic of the decisive rift between client and architect (see p. 41), and they were never built.

The present stables seem to have been built under the supervision of C. R. Cockerell. On 21 April 1846 he billed Morrison £26 5s for one day at Basildon, drawings, model and several estimates for stables. However, the stables as built show little of Cockerell's characteristic style and they seem to have been completed by David Brandon, who was also carrying out work at Basildon church, and to cottages on the estate.

Basildon and its Owners

The earliest known reference to Basildon is in 1311, when Elias de Coleshulle and his heirs were granted free warren over Coleshill, Buscot and Basildon. In the 16th and early 17th centuries the manor was owned by the Yonge family.

Bourchiers and Fanes

In 1654 Basildon became the property of the 5th Earl of Bath, Henry Bourchier (1593–1654). Bourchier died without a male heir, and in 1680 his wife left Basildon to Sir Henry Fane, her nephew and a grandson of the 1st Earl of Westmorland. Although the Fane family retained Basildon until 1771, little is known of their activities on the estate. The Gothick lodges at the entrances to the south and north-west drives were probably built during the time of the 2nd and last Viscount Fane. He may have also planted some of the trees still standing in the park today. Fane died in 1766 and the house was put up for sale by his widow and her co-heirs. Lady Fane remained at the dower house, now known as the Grotto, until her death in 1792.

The Sykes Family

Basildon Park remained on the market until 1771, when the estate was finally purchased by Francis Sykes, a newly wealthy 'nabob' (anglicised version of the Indian title 'Nawab') recently returned from India and looking to realise his political aspirations. Given its proximity to London, a manor like Basildon was eminently suitable for a wealthy and ambitious man such as Sykes. Indeed, the Berkshire area was to become home to so many British 'nabobs' that it was later referred to as 'the English Hindoostan'.

Francis Sykes was born in 1732 in the West Riding village of Thornhill, near Dewsbury. The family were distant relatives of the Sykeses of Sledmere, major landowners in the East Riding. By 1751 the young Sykes had been sent to the East India Company's factory in Kasimbazar (now in the Baharampur municipality), 100 miles from Calcutta, having joined the company the previous year as a writer. As with all company servants, he received a nominal salary; private trading and the acceptance of presents was permitted – and fortunes could be made quickly. It was here that Sykes became friends with Warren Hastings, and later became embroiled in the revolution in Bengal.

(Right) The Gothick Tower Lodge was probably built in the mid-18th century by the 2nd Viscount Fane

Siraj-ud Daula, the Nawab of Bengal, attacked Kasimbazar and Calcutta in June 1756. Sykes was among those imprisoned at Kasimbazar but he managed to escape. Clive recovered Calcutta in January 1757, and Sykes joined him before the decisive Battle of Plassey in June of that year. Regaining Calcutta had reinstated the East India Company's privileges, and Bengal became increasingly subject to British dominance. Also in that year, Sykes became Factor of Kasimbazar. He returned to England due to ill health in 1761 – the year after Clive himself returned to England seeking a political career.

Sykes had amassed a sufficient fortune to purchase Ackworth Park near Pontefract (now demolished), which remained his seat during a second and even more profitable appointment in India. The intervening years had seen further unrestrained behaviour by the remaining company merchants, and Clive returned to India in May 1765, as Governor of Bengal. In the same year, Sykes took up the positions of Chief at Kasimbazar and Resident at the Court of the Nawab of Bengal at Murshidabad. He proceeded to follow Clive's suggestion to gather some 'fair and honorable advantage'. He later

Sir Francis Sykes, builder of Basildon

accepted 'a lack or upwards in jewels' in return for commercial privileges from Muhammad Reza Khan, Collector of Revenue for Bengal. East India Company policy and governance saw him continue to profit over the next three years.

Ill health, the departure of Clive in 1767 and imminent elections may have all contributed to Sykes's return to England in 1768. Tragically, Catherine Ridley, his wife of two years, died of cholera shortly before his departure. He returned to Ackworth Park with two infant sons and quickly entered politics, becoming MP for Shaftesbury in the Duke of Grafton's administration of 1768.

(Left) This plate is part of a Chinese service (on display in the Dining Room) made for Sykes in the 1760s. It bears his coat of arms before he was made a baronet in 1781

Basildon Park, which Sykes began building in 1776, but never completed

Sykes's purchase of Basildon Park and its 2,500 acres in 1771 was probably due to his Indian connections. Lord Clive had attempted to buy it in 1767, but later settled for Claremont. Other 'nabobs' had moved into the area, including Sykes's close friend, Warren Hastings who, after retiring as Governor-General of Bengal, lived first at Beaumont near Windsor and later at Purley Hall near Pangbourne. Governor Benyon, formerley Governor of Fort St George (Madras) retired to Englefield nearby. The Vicar of Basildon, Dr George Bellasis, also had East India Company connections, and probably informed Sykes of Basildon's virtues and availability. Sykes's fortune was well invested in additional property: he retained Ackworth Park, and had purchased Motcombe House and the Gillingham Manor Estate of 2,200 acres in Dorset, along with freehold properties in Shaftesbury, in order to obtain electoral influence in that borough.

Sykes did not begin building his new house until 1776, perhaps partly due to some loss of fortune and growing political turmoil. In 1772 East India Company shares crashed, and Sykes reportedly lost £10,000 in one day. By 1773 growing alarm in Britain over the activities of the Bengal administration led to a parliamentary enquiry. Sykes wrote to Hastings on 8 November 1773, 'The debate began at three in the afternoon and continued to five in the morning in warm contest. I never suffered more in my own mind when I was a prisoner with Sr Seragah id Dowlah than I did that very night, and you may easily judge at Lord Clive's situation that he did not know that he had a sixpence to call his own in the morning.' Clive survived the debate, but committed suicide in 1774. Sykes was temporarily unseated as MP for Shaftesbury on charges of corruption, eventually paying £11,000 in damages in 1776.

Sykes's second marriage in 1774, to the 2nd Viscount Galway's daughter, Elizabeth Monckton, may have reintroduced some stability into his family life, and prompted the desire for a grander house. In 1775 he consulted

James Wyatt about Basildon, but he decided to entrust the commission to John Carr of York. Payments to Carr run from May 1777 until 1783. In 1784 the London cabinetmaker George Seddon was paid £800 for decorating the interior. By the mid-1780s, Sykes had re-established his position in society, having gained a baronetcy in March 1781 and a new parliamentary seat, as MP for Wallingford, in 1784, which he retained until his death.

Though work was still being undertaken in 1794, 'gradually completing in a style of elegance suited to the exterior appearance', the rooms on the principal floor at Basildon, notably the Octagon Drawing Room, were never finished internally as Carr had intended. This may be partly due to the worries caused by the next generation. In 1786 Sykes's younger son, then aged 21, had died at sea. The elder son, Francis William, sadly followed the route of many sons of the newly wealthy. After only two terms at Oxford, the young Francis went on the Grand Tour to Lausanne, where he took up gambling. He made sporadic efforts to lead a worthwhile life (a purchased army commission, second MP for Wallingford with his father for two years, a dutiful marriage), but more typical of his lifestyle were a notorious and expensive court case for seducing the wife of a brother officer, a duel and an inability to live within his means. He was supported by his father for a time, but fleeing his creditors, he died, along with his wife and one of his three sons, of smallpox, in Germany in 1804, seriously in debt. Sykes's daughter by his second wife married his neighbour, Richard Benyon of Englefield.

Sir Francis died in 1804 only a few weeks before his elder son. Francis William's eldest surviving son, also Francis (1799–1843), became the 3rd Baronet at the age of five. It seems that Basildon Park was already mortgaged when he inherited, and the house was let to a series of tenants, including Sir John Cam Hobhouse, the friend and executor of Lord Byron.

Benjamin Disraeli described the house as a 'Palladian palace', where between 1834 and 1835 he spent 'some romantic hours', presumably in the company of his mistress – and Sir Francis's wife – Henrietta Villebois, whom Disraeli immortalised in his 1837 novel *Henrietta Temple: A Love Story*. Sir Francis's own extravagances – living as part of the Prince of Wales's Carlton House set – had compounded the family's debts, and in 1829 he tried to sell the estate. As he refused to accept anything less then £100,000, the property remained unsold until 1838, when it was purchased for £97,000 by the art collector and Liberal MP James Morrison.

(Left) Sir Francis Sykes, 3rd Bt, with his wife Henrietta and their children; painted in romanticised medieval guise c.1837 by Daniel Maclise, who became Henrietta's lover

James Morrison

James Morrison (1789–1857) was one of the most successful merchants and richest men of the 19th century. He came from humble origins, the son of an innkeeper from Middle Wallop in Wiltshire, but his success in the haberdashery business enabled him to amass a vast fortune and estate, and to bridge the social divide that separated commerce and high society. He began his career as a 'shopman' for Messrs Todd & Co., a firm of wholesale haberdashers based at the Fore Street Warehouse in the City of London. He was so successful that in 1814 he married his employer's daughter, Anne Todd, and was quickly made a partner in the firm. Soon, he gained sole control of the business, and increased its turnover dramatically, from £64,449 in 1813 to £650,570 in 1817. His success was based in his famous dictum of 'small profits and quick returns', and one of his most celebrated business coups was to corner the market in black crêpe at the time of Queen Caroline's death in 1821.

Morrison's interests were not confined to business. He turned to the field of politics, befriending radical political and economic theorists such as Jeremy Bentham, John Stuart Mill and Richard Owen, and he entered Parliament in 1830 as the Liberal MP for St Ives. He served as Chairman of the Commons Select Committee on Railways before retiring in 1847.

Morrison was keen to realise the full potential of the railway. The building of the railway line to Reading, and the proposal to extend it below the very gates of Basildon was probably a deciding factor in his decision to buy the place. Shortly after moving here, he wrote, delighted with the prospect:

We shall soon not want a Town House. In three years all the best Physicians will recommend a ride in a steam carriage an hour before dinner as much better than a ride in the Park, and my cards will run thus; Train off at 6; dinner on table 7 precisely; return steam up at 1/2 past 10; carriages to Paddington at 1/4 past 11; Brunel and 50 miles an hour!

He was fascinated by the opportunities the new invention afforded. The fast railway journey from Basildon to London probably accounted for his eventual decision to live here rather that at the Pavilion at Fonthill in Wiltshire, which he had bought by the 1830s. He also appreciated how the railway could be used to transport goods and building materials around the country to his numerous estates. On the other hand, the railway threatened to spoil life at Basildon by coming far too close to his domain, requiring new planting to screen the track and trains from view. The building of the railway also caused him inconvenience and brought out his disputatious nature. He was even taken to court for assaulting a 'niggling specimen' of a surveyor, presumably from the railway company.

Morrison also became interested in the arts, largely through the influence of his then close friend, the architect John Buonarotti Papworth, whom he had first encountered designing handkerchiefs for Todd & Co. His initial forays into patronage and collecting seem to have been whimsical. Having just purchased Constable's *The Lock* at the Royal Academy in 1824, he wrote to Papworth, 'If I get very good at things I shall become attached to the arts, if not I shall desert them for another hobby'. In 1826 he made a grand tour with his wife. She embarked upon some commercial espionage, he made some spectacular business gambles, and they generally mixed business with a pleasurable exploration of the arts, examining 'spinning and statues – ploughing and painting – shops and cathedrals – weaving and Geology – Botany and Biblioteques'. His subsequent purchases of outstanding works of art, and his partnership with the celebrated dealer William Buchanan, ensured that his knowledge increased, and his collecting became as canny as his business acumen.

Morrison befriended many contemporary artists, including David Wilkie, from whom he bought *The Confessional* (now in the National Gallery of Scotland) in 1837, and Charles Eastlake, who painted *The Escape of the Carrara Family* for him in 1834 and later became Director of the National Gallery. It was the Eastlakes who on 30 June 1854 sent the German art historian Dr Gustav Waagen 'off this morning, with the lark, to Basildon', where he observed both of these pictures hanging amongst

*James Morrison;
pencil sketch by
Sir Francis
Chantrey, c.1842
(National Portrait
Gallery)*

other modern British pictures in the Octagon
Drawing Room.

Although a supporter of contemporary art,
Morrison also avidly collected Dutch, Flemish
and French masterpieces of the 17th century
and amassed a collection of works by artists
such as Rubens, Veronese, Steen, Hobbema
and Rembrandt. In the summer of 1838, he
purchased Rubens's *Miracle of St Francis of Paola*
from Buchanan. The following November they
collaborated to buy the entire collection of
Dutch paintings belonging to Edward Gray of
Harringey House, Hornsey for £15,000. For
the next twelve years they formed a profitable
business partnership. Buchanan had a wide network of agents in Europe, hunting out pictures,
especially in unsettled areas, such as France.
Morrison possessed the capital to finance the
deals. Buchanan would often send paintings to
Morrison's house in Harley Street, or to
Papworth, allowing Morrison to make the first
pick of the best imported pictures. Papworth
also gave advice, including the best ways of
hanging paintings by Turner and Constable,
and on the cleaning, restoration and framing of
newly acquired paintings. However, Morrison
also bought independently, and was known to

have successfully purchased, using his own
judgement, works by Van Dyck, Claude,
Greuze and Poussin.

Morrison's eye, and ability to strike a good
deal, extended into the decorative arts.
According to Waagen, his house in Harley
Street was full of 'specimens of costly plate,
vases, objects in ivory … Raphael-ware, and
other tasteful objects … quite in keeping with
the other works of art in this fine collection'.
Papworth played a pivotal role in this aspect of
Morrison's collecting, maintaining links with
some of the most celebrated antique dealers of
the period. These included Samuel Isaacs of
Regent Street, Edward Holme Baldock of
Hanway Street, and Webb and Cragg of Old
Bond Street.

Morrison's approach to the furnishing of
Basildon was also influenced by Papworth. In
September 1839, for example, Papworth, with
his son, measured up the Hall and Staircase
for carpets. He commissioned exotic Indian
furniture from G. & T. Seddon and upholstery
from Morants, calling upon a well-established
network of contacts.

On acquiring Basildon as a suitable 'casket'
for his 'pictorial gems', Morrison immediately

engaged Papworth to carry out improvements to the mansion, its parkland setting, service buildings, lodges, farms and cottages. His influence even extended to the railway bridge at Pangbourne, where Isambard Kingdom Brunel was persuaded to stop work in order to consider Morrison and Papworth's alterations.

In 1839 Papworth suggested making a terraced carriage approach to the saloon entrance. He debated whether the east wing of the house should be removed, and if not, whether a colonnade should be built. He also suggested altering the south pavilion to incorporate an area for sculpture, in place of the courtyard; a picture gallery; and elsewhere on the ground floor, the creation of an Etruscan room next to the billiard room (now the Garden Room). However, all these proposals were turned down. Most of the work which was actually carried out concerned the completion of the existing rooms which Sykes had left unfinished, and the introduction of improved services to add to the ease and comfort of life at Basildon.

Thomas Burton, who visited Basildon to prepare estimates for Papworth's work, recorded how he was 'most agreeably disappointed' by Basildon: 'I had supposed a place not merely unfinished, but *neglected for fifty years*. – It is most excellent. It is much to be regretted that Sykes could not find the wherewithal to finish the rooms for you, it would have saved you somewhere about £1000. The entire redecorating and repairing the whole of interior and exterior I write down at another £1500.' This was an optimistic figure, as his tender for the initial phase of work totalled no less than £4,080.

Hot water and a bell system were installed, and the mansion redecorated and fitted out to house Morrison's family and his collection. The decorating was carried out by Mr Simpson, who in 1843 submitted a bill for £1,239. Simpson and Burton also carried out much of the work to the Oxford Lodges and other buildings on the estate.

Papworth advised Morrison on security, suggesting that bells should be installed in the menservants' rooms, which could be operated from Morrison's bedroom, and an alarm bell fitted on the top of the house. Fire, he advised 'never occurs in a House that displays a row of Fire Buckets', because as they are passed frequently by the servants, they 'give the council *Beware of Fire*'.

Morrison filled Basildon with his famous art collection, which included Turner's painting, Thomson's Aeolian Harp *(now in Manchester City Art Gallery)*

Papworth's letters to Morrison indicate many of the usual frustrations that can accompany a major building contract. Papworth's ambitions sometimes outstripped those of his client. Despairing of the work in the Octagon Drawing Room, Mary Anne Morrison commented to her husband, 'I own I always dread Mr Papworth's love of gold and loading in decoration.' Problems arose with the introduction of new technology, and a frenzy of correspondence concerned the 'hot water affair' of 1840, which became the 'most intolerable plague' to architect and client. The newly installed boiler had been ruined because it had been fired up when empty. Papworth suspected that the system had been drained by someone of 'mischievous intention'. Morrison probably got closer to the truth when he complained that no 'instructions on the spot' were left on how to manage the system.

Morrison was an exacting client, who scrutinised both the architect's and the contractors' invoices very closely. Few bills seem to have been settled without question. Indeed, it was a dispute concerning Papworth's fees, and the time he claimed to have spent working on the stables, that resulted in the rift between the two, and a court case in which Papworth sued his old friend for outstanding expenses, and lost.

After 1842, the Morrisons spent little time at Fonthill, and with their seven sons and three daughters enjoyed a typically full Victorian family life at Basildon. Regular visitors included John Delane, the editor of *The Times*, James Wilson, founder of the *Economist*, Bishop Samuel Wilberforce, and the artist J. M. W. Turner, who wrote to Mrs Morrison: 'Mr Turner begs to present his thanks for the kind invitation to Basildon in the course of this month or the next, and hopes he may bring his fishing tackle.' Morrison complained that his neighbours were dull, and that their thinking hardly ever stretched beyond the pleasures of wine and sport. As a result, the local doctor was a more frequent dinner guest than most of the local gentry.

J. B. Papworth probably painted the Hall ceiling in its present warm tones

Charles Morrison (1818–1909)

In 1857 James Morrison's eldest son, Charles, inherited Basildon and his late father's estate on Islay. He inherited also his father's business acumen and continued to expand the firm of Morrison & Sons. He lived modestly at 93 Harley Street and at Basildon, where, apart from constructing a new lodge in Frying Pan Lane, he concentrated his building expenditure on the surrounding community, paying for a new Charity School in Lower Basildon, and a new church and Church of England infants school in Upper Basildon. He never married and had a reputation for eccentricity, reputedly walking the streets of London with his pockets turned inside out in order to convince potential thieves that he had nothing worth stealing. Despite this, he died leaving an estate valued at £10 million. Basildon Park passed to his sister, Ellen Morrison, who died only seven months after her brother.

The 20th Century

In 1910 Basildon was inherited by Charles Morrison's nephew, James, but he appears not to have occupied the house, which came to be used as a convalescent home for soldiers of the Berkshire regiments in the First World War. The next 40 years were characterised by uncertainty and a series of threats.

Major James Archibald Morrison (known as 'Jummie' to his friends) won the DSO in the First World War. According to Harold Macmillan, he was calm, courageous and intelligent, despite the fact that he was 'proud and corpulent' and insisted on walking rather than crawling when under enemy fire. Although he did not live at Basildon, Jummie invested heavily in improving the estate, commissioning Lutyens to design model villages in Upper and Lower Basildon. His flock of pedigree Hampshire Down sheep was regarded as one of the finest in the country; the Basildon Park Poultry Farms had an impressive catalogue of breeds; and pedigree shire horses and the Basildon herd of pedigree Red Poll cattle were famed for their prize-winning champions.

James Archibald Morrison had a passion for country pursuits, in particular shooting and fishing. It was at a shooting party at Basildon in 1911 that the directors of the paper company Millington & Sons reputedly coined the name 'Basildon Bond' for their new brand of writing paper. He inherited a significant fortune from both his father and his uncle, but a lavish lifestyle and three marriages seriously depleted his capital, resulting in the sale of his Basildon estate in 1928. On his death in 1934, his estate was valued at just over £5,000.

Basildon was purchased by the 1st Lord Iliffe, a publisher and newspaper proprietor, in order

to consolidate his landholdings at neighbouring Yattendon, where he had already built himself a new house. He retained the land on the western edge of the estate, and removed seven doors and two chimneypieces from the house to his London house in Carlton House Terrace. The subsequent sale of Basildon Park as a speculative lot, and its purchase by a property developer, George Ferdinando, is described on p. 3. His scheme to sell, dismantle and re-erect the house in the United States for $1 million failed. He sold some of the decorative details from the house to Crowthers, a firm specialising in architectural antiques, and elements from the Dining Room found their way to New York, where they were used to create the 'Basildon Room' at the Waldorf Astoria Hotel. But apparently Ferdinando had a change of heart about Basildon, and he lived in a wing of the house until the Second World War.

The principal portion of the house had been unoccupied for nearly 30 years when the Second World War broke out and Basildon was requisitioned. For twelve years it served a variety of purposes, all vital to the war effort, but detrimental to Basildon itself. The park was used by British soldiers to practise tank warfare, and two units of the 101st Airborne Division of the American Army completed their training here before D-Day in June 1944. After the invasion of France, they returned to Basildon to prepare for the invasion of Holland. After the war, the house became a mess for officers in charge of prisoners of war billeted in huts in the woods, and it continued to be used by the Ministry of Works to house workers constructing the Nuclear Research Establishment at Harwell. When the property was returned to Mr Ferdinando, some basic repairs were carried out. For example, the roof was rebuilt to a simplified and cheaper design above the Great Staircase, where the lead had been stolen by the Ministry of Works caretaker. However, the property was returned in a very poor state of repair, suffering from the loss of details and the effects of twelve years' intensive use. The future looked bleak, as extensive work was required at a time of strict controls on building materials. Basildon seemed about to share the fate of many other houses at this time, sliding gradually towards dereliction and demolition.

(Right) The 'Basildon Room' in the Waldorf Astoria in New York incorporates decorative plasterwork removed from the house

(Left) During the First World War, Basildon was used as a convalescent home for wounded soldiers

The Iliffes

Meanwhile, Lord Iliffe's elder son, the Hon. Langton Iliffe, had in 1938 married Renée Merandon du Plessis, who had been born and brought up in an old British colonial house on a sugar estate in Mauritius. Lady Iliffe left the island when she was fifteen, and spent much time with her aunt in Paris and her grandfather in Versailles. She regards this as a formative period, with every Saturday spent admiring the park at Versailles. The couple lived at first in London at Carlton House Terrace and at the Little Malthouse at Yattendon. Before the war they had looked at Baddesley Clinton, a romantic moated manor house in Warwickshire that dated back to the 15th century (now also in the care of the National Trust). However, the outbreak of the war in 1939 put an end to these plans. After the war, they began to search for a house in the country. It should be close to the Yattendon estate and preferably Georgian, since they were developing a shared love of 18th-century art and architecture. Basildon was a larger house than they had first envisaged, yet in every other respect it seemed to fit the bill, and in 1952 they made the courageous decision to buy and restore it.

It is now 50 years since the Iliffes decided to embark upon the restoration of Basildon, and nearly 25 years since they gave it to the National Trust. How they set about this huge task can be seen not only as a chapter in the history of Basildon, but also as part of the history of 20th-century taste, and it is fascinating to analyse how the two interlock. Restoring the damaged decoration of the rooms and acquiring pictures and furniture resulted in an ensemble both appropriate to the house, yet also expressive of the enthusiasms of their times.

By the First World War, Georgian taste was already beginning to offer a fashionable alternative to Victorian England and its aftermath. For the novelist Evelyn Waugh, the Georgian era represented an aesthetic of orderliness, preferable to the clichés of 'Ye Olde Englande' favoured by his father. For others, it was sufficiently far removed from modern memory to be worthy of study by the connoisseur and scholar. The Magnasco Society was formed in 1924 by the Sitwells, Lord Gerald Wellesley and Christopher Hussey to enjoy and promote the Italian collections of the 18th-century grand tourist. The Georgian Group was founded in 1937 to campaign for the preservation of the buildings of this era.

By the middle of the century a host of publications, both scholarly and popular, promoted the history, houses, arts, gardens and ideas of 18th-century England. Works by

Renée, Lady Iliffe; painted by Frank O. Salisbury in c. 1942 (Great Staircase)

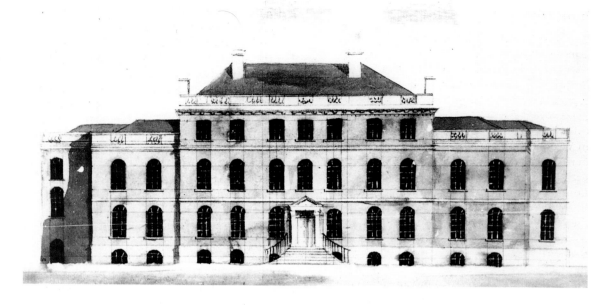

Christopher Hussey, Ralph Dutton, Margaret Jourdain and Sacheverell Sitwell can be found amongst the volumes in the Iliffes' library. They provided a starting point for what developed into a very personal and forward-looking interpretation of Georgian taste and informed the Iliffes' restoration of Basildon.

A network of friends and dealers helped the Iliffes educate themselves about the architecture of Basildon, and the furnishings that would be suitable for it. They were advised by the architect Winton Aldridge and they visited many of Carr's houses to discover more about the original architect of the house. On their travels, they discovered Panton Hall in Lincolnshire, a fascinating house, designed by Talman, finished by Hawksmoor and subsequently refitted by Carr, which was derelict by the 1950s.

The Iliffes regularly attended the salerooms of Sotheby's and Christie's, often choosing the less fashionable auctions to gain a wider feel for the market. Lord Iliffe acquired a collection of old, annotated catalogues, and marked up his own with notes and prices so that he could keep a track of market trends. The Iliffes also attended many of the great country-house dispersal sales of the time. At the Ashburnham Place sale in 1953 they purchased the fine suite of the state bed, curtains and furniture now in the Crimson

(Above) Panton Hall in Lincolnshire, another derelict Carr of York house from which the Iliffes salvaged fittings for Basildon

(Below) The Iliffes refurnished Basildon with English and French pieces of the highest quality. This armchair is believed to have belonged to Princess Amelia, the favourite daughter of George III

The Shell Room. The present decoration was designed by Gordon Davies in 1978 to provide a backdrop for the shell collection

Bedroom, along with many other items. This sale had a great impact on many influential decorators, including Nancy Lancaster and John Fowler.

The Iliffes were aware of other mid-20th-century attempts to put a soul back into a Georgian house, such as Ralph Dutton's Georgian revival of Hinton Ampner in Hampshire. They also knew Ditchley Park in Oxfordshire, which had been sold in 1933 to Mr and Mrs Ronald Tree, whose decoration of this great 18th-century house was influential on both sides of the Atlantic. The Trees' Anglo-American appreciation of 18th-century French taste resulted in a careful balance of French and English influences, which provides an interesting parallel to the Iliffes' subtle blend of the same styles at Basildon. There are a number of other parallels. The Iliffes collected in a similar manner to the Trees, buying many objects in English country-house sales. Both the Iliffes and the Trees concentrated their efforts on purchases which were appropriate to their respective houses, yet neither couple was a slave to style or date. Lord Iliffe, as Ronnie Tree had done, developed a finely tuned enthusiasm for works of art, fine furniture and objects, whilst Lady Iliffe, like Mrs Tree, developed a lightness of touch and a gift for arrangement that brought the house to life. When Ditchley was sold, the Iliffes attended the sale and purchased a number of items, including a carpet, side-tables and the bed now to be seen in the Green Chintz Room.

The Iliffes showed a great skill in reinterpreting the atmosphere and detail of the

Georgian house, and Lady Iliffe was particularly ingenious in reusing old and sometimes unlikely materials to create a warm, mellow and harmonious effect. Her upbringing in an old Mauritian colonial house may have given her a special sensitivity to old buildings, whilst the shortages of post-war Britain clearly dictated the ingenious frugality which characterises much of the interior decoration at Basildon. For example, the grand curtains in Lady Iliffe's Bedroom were made by Lady Iliffe herself, using utilitarian tapes and wool to impressive effect. Because so many historic houses were facing dispersal and demolition in the 1950s, large quantities of upholstery materials were becoming available. In many ways, the Iliffes' approach was forward-looking. They resisted the temptation to do a complete 'makeover', and respected the character and patina of the house. It was not until more recently that the importance and role of older materials in the decoration of historic houses have been fully recognised.

The decoration and arrangement of Basildon were carried out almost exclusively by Lady Iliffe. She was particularly skilled at creating a rich style with economy. For example, in the

The painted top of the c.1820 table in the Hall

The Red Bathroom. The striking décor was created by the Iliffes

Octagon Drawing Room, she lined the walls with red felt, following a French tradition of putting fabric on the walls. The richly carved pelmet boards from Ashburnham Place complemented the richness of Papworth's 19th-century scheme, and provided an admirable backdrop for Lord Iliffe's Italian paintings.

The only professional interior designer to be used was John Fowler, who was equally adept at making do with limited resources. Fowler's work at Basildon was confined to creating a blue drawing room in what is now the Dining Room. It has been replaced by the scheme created by Lady Iliffe's nephew-in-law, Alec Cobbe. However, the cream chintz with a yellow geometrical pattern that Fowler supplied remains in the Octogan Drawing Room.

The picture collection which the Iliffes assembled mirrored the development of English taste in the mid-20th century. Lord Iliffe initially concentrated on French Impressionist paintings of a scale suitable for their home in Yattendon. The purchase of Basildon dictated a major change, for the scale, proportion and period of the house demanded a very different type of painting. Lord Iliffe began to form a collection

Rebecca at the Well; by the early 18th-century Italian artist Sebastiano Galeotti. The Iliffes led the revival of interest in such works

in the spirit of the great picture-collecting contemporaries of Sir Francis Sykes, but with a subtle difference. This is most evident in his purchase of Batoni's series of paintings of the Apostles. Batoni was celebrated amongst the English visitors to Rome in the 1760s as a portrait-painter, yet Lord Iliffe's collection shows him as a religious artist – an aspect of his career not represented in Britain until the 1950s. Lady Iliffe has recorded how she admired the Roman quality of the paintings, and felt them to be far superior to a collection of portraits 'of other peoples' ancestors'. Lord Iliffe also patronised contemporary artists, most notably Graham Sutherland (see p. 12).

Lord Iliffe was advised by a number of dealers and art historians. Just after the Second World War, the Iliffes met Francis Egerton, a director of Mallets who became a close friend and mentor. Just after the Second World War. Dudley Tooth gave advice about French Impressionist paintings, and was prepared to trade them in for Italian Old Masters. Later, Trenchard Cox and Mary Woodhall of Birmingham City Art Gallery introduced the Iliffes to the dealers Colnaghi and Agnews, who sold them Old Masters. The Iliffes also made regular visits to exhibitions: particularly influential was *English Taste in the Eighteenth Century*, held at the Royal Academy in 1955–6. It was also a period when pictures of the highest quality could be purchased for reasonable sums. The inflated prices of the modern art market prohibit such an approach today.